T0145025

Beyond The Manger

BRENDA BUCKNER

WestBow Press books may be ordered through booksellers or by contacting:

WestBow Press
A Division of Thomas Nelson & Zondervan
1663 Liberty Drive
Bloomington, IN 47403
www.westbowpress.com
844-714-3454

Scripture quotations marked NKJV are taken from the New King James Version®.
Copyright © 1982 by Thomas Nelson. Used by permission. All rights reserved.

Scripture quotations marked ICB are taken from The Holy Bible, International Children's
Bible® Copyright© 1986, 1988, 1999, 2015 by Thomas Nelson. Used by permission.

ISBN: 978-1-6642-9802-6 (sc)
ISBN: 978-1-6642-9803-3 (e)

Library of Congress Control Number: 2023907291

Print information available on the last page.

WestBow Press rev. date: 04/27/2023

WESTBOW
PRESS®
A DIVISION OF THOMAS NELSON
& ZONDERVAN

This book is dedicated first to our Lord and Savior Jesus Christ. I would also like to dedicate this book to my six precious grandchildren: Kendall, Ezekiel, Lyric, Camden, Braylen and Armani, along with every precious child the Lord has ever created.

This story begins on a cold Christmas Eve night, with a blind grandfather sitting by the fireplace in his old rocker, smoking his corncob pipe. Suddenly, his precious little granddaughter runs to him and jumps in his lap, handing him a book and saying with excitement, "Grandpa, will you read me a bedtime story?"

Her three older brothers were playing on the floor nearby, and they started to giggle and say in a low voice, "Read! Don't she know that grandpa is blind? He can't read!"

Grandpa hears them and chuckles. He tells the children, "Yes, grandpa is blind, but this story is written on my heart, this story is written on my soul. Grandpa opens the book, pretending to read it, and begins to tell the story of *Beyond The Manger.*

'Twas the night that Jesus was born, and all through the land, not a creature was stirring, Oh no, not even a man!

The Scriptures were laid upon the shelf with such care, but nobody cared that they were lying there.

The youth were all nestled and snug in their beds, while visions of Joel 2:28 danced in their heads.

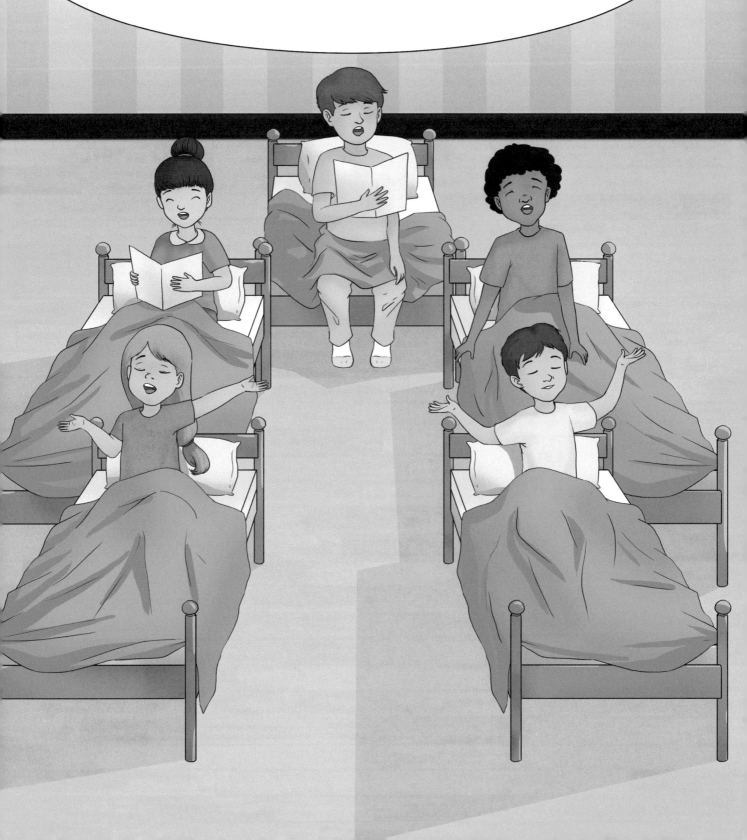

While mama was on her knees and daddy was in God's Word they both settled down to see what they thought they had just heard!

You see, out in the field there was such a shatter, they both ran to the window to see what was the matter. Away to the window they flew like a flash! Mama tore open the shutters, while daddy threw up the sash!

With the moon and the stars shining bright in the sky, there would be one star that caught both of their eyes!

Then what to their wondering eyes would appear, but a host of angels proclaiming to some shepherds, "Your Savior is here!"

The angels told the shepherds, "Go, and go quick! See the Savior that has been born; Oh no, no, not Saint Nick!"

When the angels left, the shepherds went in a flash
with their orders in hand, despite of themselves!

When they arrived to the stable, it was just as the angels had said. They saw Mary, Joseph and baby Jesus, who was tucked away in His bed!

But this bed was not a bed fit for The KING. Haha, can you imagine such a strange thing?

After the shepherds saw Jesus, they ran to spread the word, "The KING of Kings is here! Haven't you heard?"

All who heard were simply amazed, and they too spread *the Good News* all of their days!

They all glorified His Name, because the One who was foretold of is now the One who would proclaim!

Jesus came into the world to save the sinner. Repent and be baptized in his name because what he has spoken to You; OH NO, it is not a game!

You see, people of every tribe, language, people and nation, Christ is returning SOON, so I beg you to please be ready, because it could be before NOON!

"For God so loved the world that He gave His only begotten Son, that whoever believes in Him should not perish but have everlasting life. For God did not send His Son into the world to condemn the world, but that the world through Him might be saved."

John 3:16–17 (NKJV)

Printed in the United States
by Baker & Taylor Publisher Services